Country ABCs

Guatemala ABCs

A Book About the People and Places of

by Marcie Aboff ~ illustrated by Zachary Trover

Special thanks to our advisers for their expertise:
Paula Worby, Researcher and Guatemala Specialist
Berkeley, California

Susan Kesselring, M.A., Literacy Educator
Rosemount–Apple Valley–Eagan (Minnesota) School District

PICTURE WINDOW BOOKS
Minneapolis, Minnesota

...an
...acy Davies
...or: Keith Griffin
...Director: Carol Jones
...illustrations in this book were created in watercolors.

Picture Window Books
1710 Roe Crest Drive
North Mankato, MN 56003
877-845-8392
www.capstonepub.com

Library of Congress Cataloging-in-Publication Data
Aboff, Marcie.
Guatemala ABCs : a book about the people and places of
Guatemala / by Marcie Aboff ; illustrated by Zachary
Trover.
p. cm. — (Country ABCs)
Includes bibliographical references and index.
ISBN: 978-1-4048-1570-4 (library binding)
ISBN: 978-1-4048-1918-4 (paperback)
1. Guatemala—Juvenile literature. 2. Alphabet books. I.
Trover, Zachary. II. Title. III. Series.
F1463.2.A26 2005
972.81—dc22   2005021812

Printed in the United States of America in North Mankato, Minnesota.
052013   007340R

Hola! (OH-la)

That is how people say "Hello!" in Guatemala. About the size of the state of Ohio, Guatemala is the third largest country in Central America. More than 12 million people live there. With its mild climate, deep green forests, and colorful flowers and birds, Guatemala is often called the "Land of Eternal Spring."

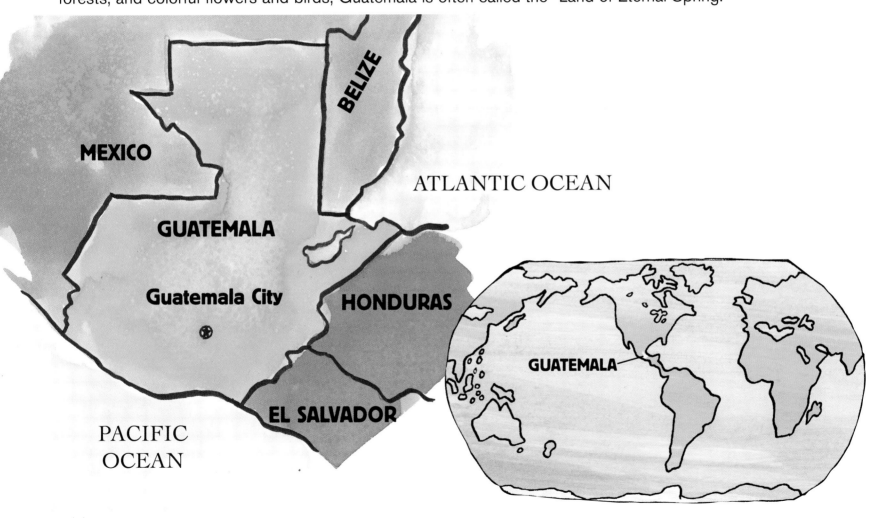

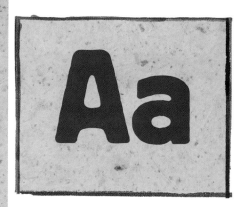

A is for art.

Ancient Mayan artists painted palace walls with murals showing battle scenes and ceremonies. They also created small, carved sculptures and beautifully decorated pottery. Guatemalan artists today use people at home, at work, or at the market as their subjects.

B is for bus.

Fewer than 3 percent of all Guatemalans own a car. Most people travel by bus instead. Guatemala has many highways and paved roads. But small towns mostly have dirt roads. During the rainy season, the roads turn to mud, making travel difficult.

Fast Fact: Horses and bicycles are common forms of transportation in the Guatemalan countryside. Many people, however, prefer to travel long distances on foot.

C is for coffee.

Guatemala produces more coffee than any other country in Central America. Coffee beans are one of the nation's most important crops. Guatemalan coffee is known throughout the world for its spicy, smoky flavor.

Fast Fact: Coffee trees produce cherry-like fruit. Farmers pick the fruit and then remove the seeds, which are called coffee beans. It takes about 4,000 beans to make 1 pound (450 grams) of coffee.

D is for Day of the Dead.

On November 1 and 2, Guatemalans celebrate the Day of the Dead. During this holiday, people think about family members who have died. They decorate gravesites with flowers. They share bowls of *fiambre* (fee-AHM-bray), a salad made of cold meats and vegetables.

Fast Fact: In the town of Santiago Saquetepéquez, people build and fly huge kites for the Day of the Dead. Some kites are more than 20 feet (6 meters) across. The kites are meant to show the connection between the living and the dead.

7

E is for ethnicity.

Guatemalans come from many different ethnicities. People from the largest ethnic group, called Ladinos or Mestizos, are of mixed Spanish and Indian background. They use Spanish as their first language. Guatemalans of Mayan descent (the second largest ethnic group) are called Maya or Mayan Indians. Like the ancient Maya, many Mayan people today are farmers.

Fast Fact: Even though Spanish is Guatemala's official language, about 20 Mayan languages are also spoken throughout the country. Mayan children learn Spanish when they go to school.

8

F is for flag.

The Guatemalan flag has three wide, vertical stripes. The light blue stripes on the left and right stand for the Pacific Ocean and the Atlantic Ocean. The Guatemalan coat of arms on the white, middle stripe features the quetzal, Guatemala's national bird. The bird stands for freedom.

G is for Guatemala City.

Most city dwellers live in and around Guatemala City, the nation's capital. About 1 million people live in Guatemala City. Close to 3 million people live in the surrounding areas. Guatemala City is the country's center of government, finance, industry, music, and theater.

H is for Holy Week.

Guatemala's most important Catholic celebrations are held during the seven days before Easter Sunday. This week is called "Holy Week," or *Semana Santa* (say-MAH-na SAHN-ta). People walk in processions carrying huge, decorated platforms. These platforms honor saints and key events in Jesus' life.

Fast Fact: During Holy Week, many Catholics create designs on the streets. They use colored pine needles, flower petals, and dyed sawdust.

11

I is for ice cream.

When Guatemalans want ice cream, they listen for bells. Bell-ringing ice-cream carts are common on city and town streets, especially on hot days and holidays. Frozen fruit juices are another popular sweet treat. They're often sold in small, clear, plastic bags.

Jj

J is for jade.

The single most prized material for ancient Mayan artists was jade. Many examples of jade jewelry have been found in Mayan tombs. Jade has even been found in teeth—a mark of wealth. Today, Guatemalans mine a very hard kind of jade called jadeite.

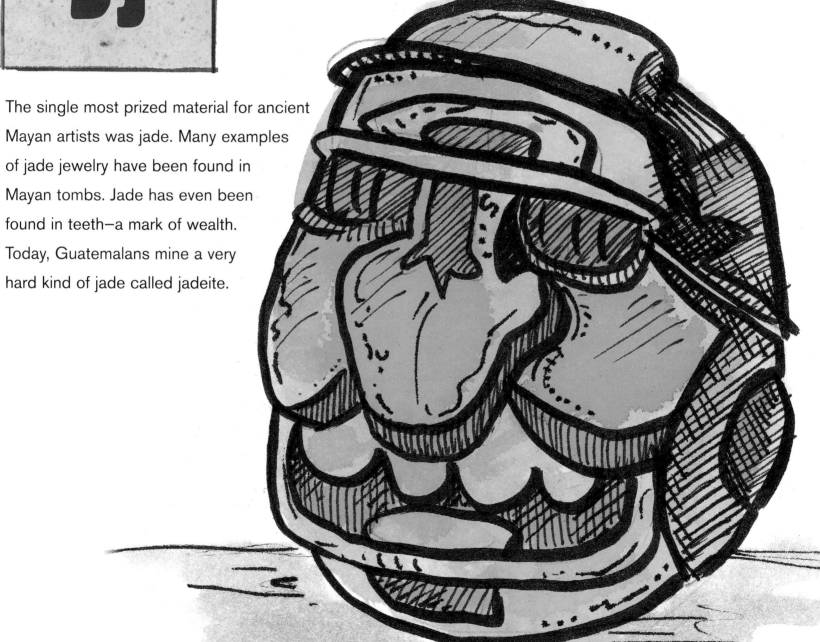

K is for Kinich Ahau.

The ancient Maya worshipped many gods. The Sun God was known as Kinich Ahau. Kinich Ahau was usually shown with jaguar-like features. He was considered a friendly, peace-loving god who brought light, warmth, health, and happiness to the Maya.

L is for Lake Atitlán.

Located in the mountains of southwestern Guatemala, Lake Atitlán is often called the most beautiful lake in the world. It is a brilliant blue color. Three large volcanoes border its southern shores. They are reflected in the lake's mirror-like waters.

Fast Fact: Lake Atitlán is a popular place for locals and tourists to swim, fish, and go boating. Farmers grow coffee on the volcanoes' steep slopes.

15

M is for Mayan Civilization.

The great Mayan Civilization reached its peak around A.D. 600. The ancient Maya were expert craftspeople. They built massive pyramids of stone. Some, such as those in Tikal, in northern Guatemala, held religious temples. Tikal was once the capital of the Mayan Civilization.

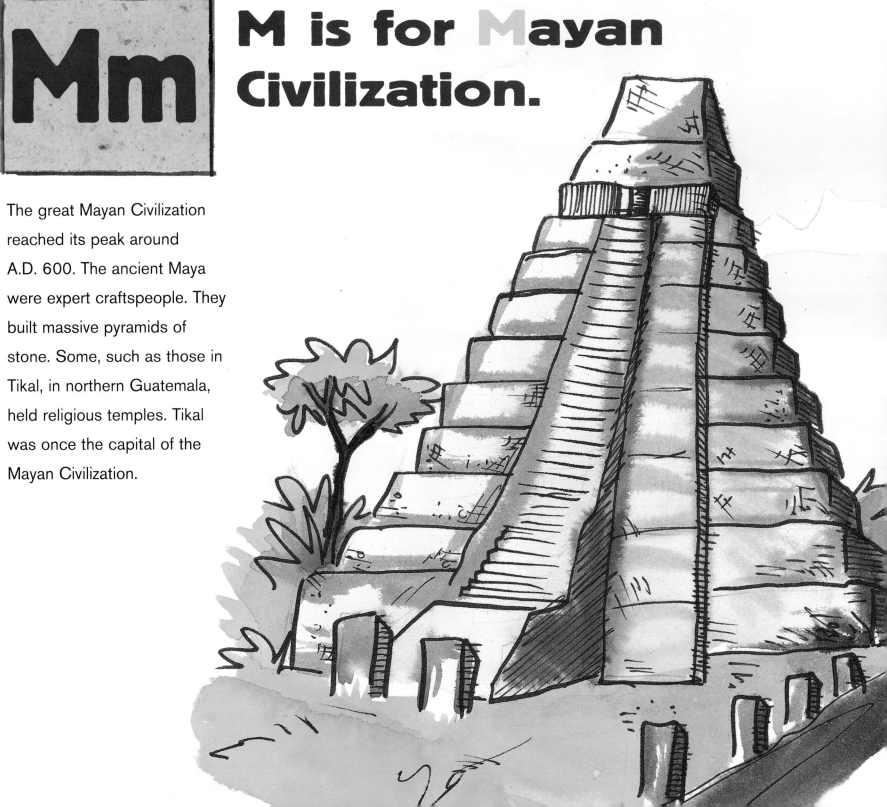

N is for nahual (NAH-wall).

Nahuals are spirit companions—similar to guardian angels. Like their ancestors, some Mayan people today believe nahuals move alongside them at all times. Nahuals are usually animals, such as jaguars, eagles, or snakes. A person's birthday determines what form his or her nahual will take.

17

O is for orchid.

Oo

Guatemala's national flower is the white nun orchid. It is so named because the blossom's outline looks like a nun in a traditional headpiece. There are more than 600 kinds of orchids in the world. Several of them grow only in Guatemala.

P is for peace.

Pp

From 1960 to 1996, Guatemala suffered from violence. People clashed with the government because not all citizens were being treated equally. Thousands of people died. However, in 1996, peace accords, or agreements, were signed. These accords promised health care, education, and other basic services to all Guatemalan citizens. Today, the people of Guatemala continue to work hard to keep the peace and improve their way of life.

Fast Fact: *Paz* is the Spanish word for "peace."

19

Q is for quetzal.

The quetzal is Guatemala's national bird. Quetzals are known for their brilliant colors and long tail feathers. Unfortunately, due to illegal hunting and the destruction of their jungle homes, quetzals are in danger of dying out.

Fast Fact: Guatemala's money is named after the quetzal bird. One hundred cents, called centavos, equal one quetzal.

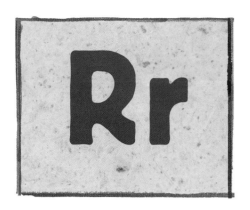

R is for rain forest.

Guatemalan rain forests are home to thousands of different kinds of animals, birds, and plants. Monkeys and tropical birds live high in the treetops. Jaguars, ocelots, and raccoon-like coatis creep down below. Rain forests receive more than 80 inches (203 centimeters) of rain each year.

Ss

S is for soccer.

Soccer is the most popular sport in Guatemala. Local soccer league teams can be found throughout the country. Guatemalan children, especially boys, play soccer from a very young age.

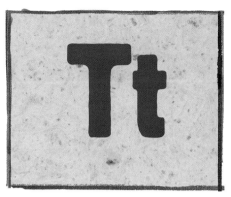

T is for tortilla (tor-TEE-yah).

Corn tortillas are typically served at every meal in Guatemala. To make tortillas, people boil corn and grind it into a paste-like dough. They roll the dough into balls, then pat and slap them until they look like thin pancakes. Finally, the tortillas are cooked on a dry griddle and eaten hot.

Fast Fact: Beans, especially black beans, are another traditional food of daily life in Guatemala. Beans are served in many different ways; for example, as soup, with rice, or ground and refried.

23

U is for unity.

Most Guatemalan towns have at least one market day each week. On market day, people from many different backgrounds and locations unite, or come together, to sell food or homemade crafts. They also shop, swap news, meet old friends, and make new ones.

Fast Fact: When other transportation is unavailable or too expensive, Guatemalans travel to market on foot. Often walking for hours, people carry heavy loads on their heads or backs.

V is for volcanoes.

A string of major volcanoes lies across southwestern Guatemala. Some are inactive. Others are active and carefully watched so that people can be ready for eruptions. Volcanic eruptions can spew ash and lava for miles.

Fast Fact: Most of the world's volcanic eruptions and earthquakes happen in a belt-like area by the Pacific Ocean. Scientists call this loop the "Ring of Fire." Guatemala's Pacific coast is part of this dangerous area.

W is for weaving.

One of the most important Mayan crafts is weaving. The brightly colored woven cloth helps to preserve an ancient Mayan tradition. It is also an important source of income for many Guatemalans.

Fast Fact: The traditional clothing worn by many Mayan people is called *traje* (TRA-hay). People from different villages weave their own unique colors and designs into their traje.

26

X is for Xelajú (shay-la-HOO).

Once known as Xelajú, Quezaltenango is Guatemala's second largest city. About 150,000 people live there. Called Xela (SHAY-la) by locals, the city is famous for its many marimba craftspeople, musicians, and composers. The marimba, a xylophone-like instrument, is the most beloved musical instrument in Guatemala.

27

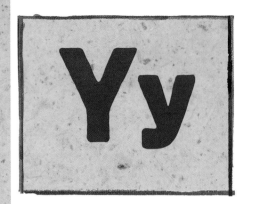

Y is for yucca (YOO-ka).

Yucca plants originated in Guatemala and Mexico. Their long, thin leaves were traditionally used for weaving and making twine. Some kinds of yuccas can grow up to 20 feet (6 meters) or more, but most are much shorter.

Fast Fact: Some cooks serve yucca flowers with their dishes. The large, bell-shaped flowers make a beautiful garnish, and they are also full of vitamins and minerals.

Z is for Zacapa (za-KAH-pa).

The desert-like Zacapa region of eastern Guatemala is known for its *sandias* (sahn-DEE-ahs; watermelons) and tamarind fruit. The odd-looking cashew fruit also grows there. It produces cashew nuts.

Guatemala in Brief

Official name: Republic of Guatemala

Capital: Guatemala City

Official language: Spanish

Population: 12 million people

People: 55 percent Ladinos/Mestizos (mixed Spanish and Indian origin); 40 percent Maya (indigenous); 5 percent Carib (African origin)

Main religions: 60 percent Roman Catholic; 30 percent Protestant; 10 percent traditional Mayan beliefs and other groups

Education: Six years of primary school are offered, followed by six years of secondary school. Less than one-third of all children attend secondary school. About one-third of all Guatemalans age 15 and older cannot read or write.

Major holidays: Holy Week (week before and including Easter; March/April); Independence Day (September 15); Day of the Dead (November 1 and 2); Christmas Day (December 25)

Transportation: buses, cars, bicycles, horses

Climate: tropical (hot, humid) in lowlands; cooler in highlands

Area: 42,042 square miles (108,889 square kilometers)

Highest point: Volcan Tajumulco, 13,845 feet (4,220 meters) above sea level

Lowest point: sea level

Type of government: democratic

Head of government: president

Major industries: processing of food, tobacco, and sugar; manufacturing of textiles and clothes

Natural resources: fertile soil, lead, nickel, zinc, copper, silver

Major agricultural products: coffee beans, bananas, corn, beans

Chief exports: coffee, bananas, sugar, cotton

National bird: quetzal

National flower: white nun orchid

Money: quetzal

Say It in SPANISH

good morning . . . . *buenos dias* (BWAY-nos DEE-ahs)

good evening . . . . *buenas noches* (BWAY-nahs NO-chez)

good-bye . . . . *adios* (ah-dee-OHS)

please . . . . *por favor* (POR fa-VOR)

thank you . . . . *gracias* (GRAH-see-ahs)

house . . . . *casa* (KAH-sa)

mother . . . . *madre* (MAH-dray)

father . . . . *padre* (PAH-dray)

Glossary

archeology—the study of human life from long ago

Catholic—someone who believes in Catholicism, a Christian religion; Christians believe that Jesus was the son of God

composers—people who write music

ethnicity—a group of people who share the same physical features, beliefs, and backgrounds

habitat—the place where an animal or plant lives

lava—melted rock that oozes or is thrown from a volcano

Mayan—belonging to the Maya, a group of people native to Central America

mine—to dig up

murals—artistic scenes painted directly on walls

processions—groups of people walking in a slow, orderly way

To Learn More

More Books to Read

Delgado, Kevin. *Guatemala.* Farmington Hills, Mich.: Lucent Books, 2005.

Dendinger, Roger. *Guatemala.* New York: Chelsea House Publishers, 2004.

Markel, Rita. *Guatemala in Pictures.* Minneapolis: Lerner Publishing, 2004.

Shields, Charles J. *Guatemala.* Broomall, Penn.: Mason Crest Publishers, 2003.

On the Web

FactHound offers a safe, fun way to find Web sites related to topics in this book. All of the sites on FactHound have been researched by our staff.

1. Visit *www.facthound.com*
2. Type in this special code: 1404815708
3. Click on the FETCH IT button.

Your trusty FactHound will fetch the best sites for you!

Index

LOOK FOR ALL OF THE BOOKS IN THE COUNTRY ABCS SERIES:

Australia ABCs
Canada ABCs
China ABCs
Egypt ABCs
France ABCs
Germany ABCs
Guatemala ABCs
India ABCs
Israel ABCs
Italy ABCs
Japan ABCs
Kenya ABCs
Mexico ABCs
New Zealand ABCs
Russia ABCs
The United States ABCs